First Science

Make it Move!

Editorial planning: Serpentine Editorial
Scientific consultant: Dr. J.J.M. Rowe

Designed by The R & B Partnership
Illustrator: David Anstey
Photographer: Peter Millard

Additional photographs:
ZEFA 6, 19; The Hutchison Library 30 (bottom);
Chris Fairclough Colour Library 9;
Stephen Dalton/NHPA 18;
Peter Millard Library 14.

Library of Congress Cataloging-in-Publication Data

Rowe, Julian.
    Make it move! / by Julian Rowe and Molly Perham.
      p.   cm. — (First science)
    Includes index.
    Summary: Describes in simple terms different ways of moving, including
pushing, lifting, pulling, swimming, flying, and rolling.
      ISBN 0-516-08135-7
      1. Force and energy—Experiments—Juvenile literature. [1. Force and energy—
Experiments. 2. Experiments.] I. Perham, Molly. II. Title. III. Series: First science
(Chicago, Ill.)
QC73.4.R68 1993
531'.6—dc20   93-13737
                                                                                    CIP
                                                                                    AC

Make it Move!

Julian Rowe
and Molly Perham

CP CHILDRENS PRESS®

CHICAGO

Contents

KITES AND BALLS page 6

PUSHING page 8

LIFTING page 10

PULLING page 12

MOVING WATER page 14

SWIMMING page 16

FLYING page 18

GLIDING page 20

WHEELS page 22

 MAKE A BOTTLE
TRACTOR page 24

STOPPING page 26

MOVING FOR FUN
page 28

THINK ABOUT...
MOVING page 30

INDEX page 32

 SAFETY WARNING

Activities marked with this symbol require the presence and
help of an adult. Plastic should always be used instead of glass.

Kites and balls

On a windy day, a kite flies high in the sky. This boy runs into the wind, pulling on the kite string. The wind pushes the kite up into the air.

Three boys are running after a ball. One of them has just kicked it. The ball shoots forward faster than the running boys.

You can also make a ball move fast by hitting it with a bat. When this girl catches the baseball, it will stop moving.

Pushing

These two girls on roller skates are pushing against each other. Which way do you think they will move?

A boat like this one floats right on top of the water. The engine can push it along very fast.

Lifting

The bag is too heavy for these boys to lift off the ground! They can hardly make it move.

Make a lever

Materials: A ruler, a small wooden block, and a can of baked beans.

Put the block under the middle of the ruler. Stand the can at one end of the ruler. Push down on the other end.

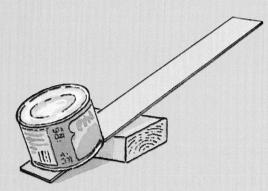

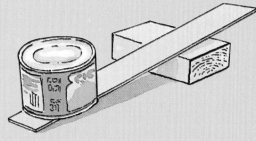

What happens if you slide the block nearer one end?

What happens if you slide it nearer the other end?

Pulling

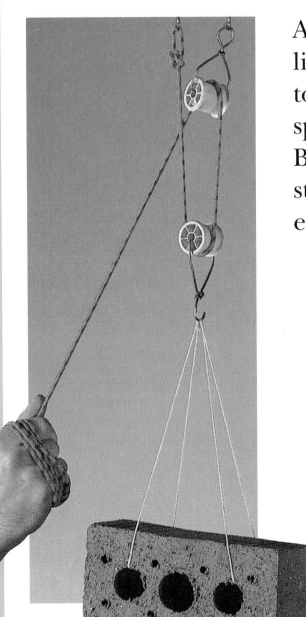

Another way to lift a heavy load is to use pulleys. The spools are pulleys. By pulling on the string, the brick is easily raised.

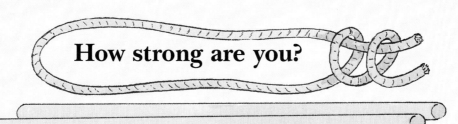

How strong are you?

Materials: Two broom handles and a piece of rope.

Tie the rope to the middle of one handle.

Ask a friend to hold this broom handle with both hands. Ask another friend to hold the other handle. Now loop the rope around both broom handles.

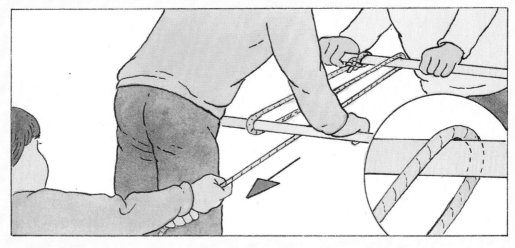

Pull on the rope.   What happens?

Moving water

Pushing and pulling make things move. Pushes and pulls are called forces. The force of the falling water turns this waterwheel. The waterwheel turns a grindstone that grinds corn to make flour.

What else are waterwheels used for?

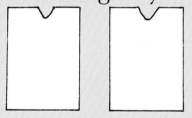

Make a waterwheel

Scissors

Materials: Six strips of thin cardboard, a knitting needle, and some modeling clay.

Attach four strips of cardboard to the knitting needle using the modeling clay.

Cut notches in the other two pieces of cardboard.

Stand the waterwheel under a faucet. Support it firmly with modeling clay. Now turn on the water gently.

Can you make the waterwheel turn fast?

Swimming

Can you swim? This girl is using her legs and arms to move through the water.

Fish move their tails from side to side to push themselves through the water.

Flying

Birds use their powerful wing muscles to fly. They flap their wings up and down to push themselves through the air.

Powerful engines push this jet airplane forward. The wings help lift it up into the sky.

Gliding

Some seeds have wings. They move through the air like a glider. This boy has thrown a handful of seeds into the air. They glide and spin to the ground.

Make a hovercraft

Materials: A large paper plate, a pencil, and a balloon.

Make a hole with the pencil in the middle of the plate.

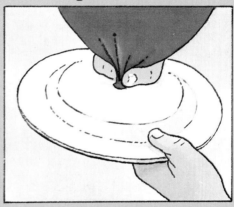

Blow up the balloon. Hold the end very tightly and push it through the hole in the plate.

Place the hovercraft on a smooth floor, and give it a push. Watch it glide away.

Can you hear the air escaping from the balloon as it glides along?

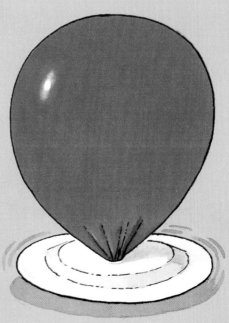

Wheels

To make the bicycle move forward, this boy
pushes on the pedals with his feet. He steers
by moving the handlebars. When he
wants to stop,
he squeezes
the brakes.

Gear wheels move round and round.
How many gear wheels has this boy put
together? Can you see what will happen
when he turns the big red wheel?

Make a bottle tractor

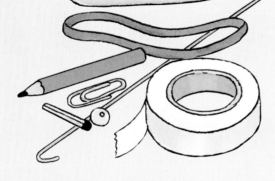

Materials:
A plastic bottle
with a screw-on top,
a large rubber band,
a pencil, a paper clip,
a match, a bead,
a long piece of wire,
and tape.

Ask an adult to make
a small hole in the
bottom of the bottle
and another in its top.

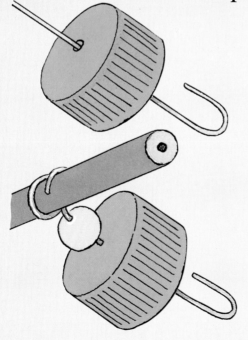

Straighten the paper
clip and push it
through the hole in
the top. Then bend
it to make a hook for
the rubber band.

Thread the bead
onto the clip, and
then wrap the clip
around the pencil.

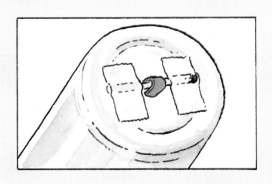

Push the rubber band through the hole in the bottom of the bottle, and fix it in place with the match and tape.

Loop the other end of the band onto the paper-clip hook, using the bent piece of wire.

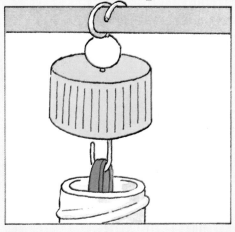

Screw on the bottle top. Turn the pencil to wind up the rubber band.

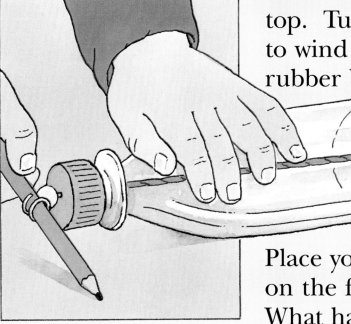

Place your tractor on the floor. What happens?

Stopping

The boy in front has stopped suddenly.
All the other children try to stop too.
What do you think happens?

Which of these shoes would be best for walking on a slippery surface?

To stop a moving bicycle, the rider squeezes the brakes.

The brakes grip the rim of the wheel, and the wheel stops moving around.

Moving for fun

Have you ever slid down a water slide? These girls are hitting the water with a great splash. Why do you think they moved so fast?

This girl holds on to the chains of the swing
as she moves her legs to swing back and forth.
She uses the muscles in her arms and legs to
make the swing go higher and higher.

Think about... moving

You have to push hard to knead dough. The harder this boy works the easier it becomes to form the dough into different shapes.

People in Egypt use a lever to lift water from rivers. This machine is called a *shadoof.*

Oil keeps things from sticking together. A bicycle wheel turns much faster when it is oiled. Oil is very slippery.

Is it easier to push a box of toys over a carpet or over a tiled floor?

INDEX

air, 6, 18, 20, 21
airplane, 19
arms, 16, 29
bag, 10
baseball, 7
bat, 7
bicycle, 22, 27, 31
birds, 18
boat, 9
brakes, 22, 27
brick, 12
bucket, 30
dough, 30
engine, 9, 19
fish, 17
football, 7
forces, 14
gear wheels, 23
gliding, 20, 21
grindstone, 14
handlebars, 22
heavy load, 10, 12
hitting, 7
hovercraft, 21
kicking, 7

kite, 6
kneading, 30
legs, 16, 29
lever, 11, 30
oil, 31
pedals, 22
pulleys, 12
pulling, 6, 12, 13, 14, 22, 27
pushing, 6, 8, 9, 11, 14, 17, 18, 19, 22, 30, 31
roller skates, 8
seeds, 20
shadoof, 30
shoes, 27
sky, 6, 19
spools, 12
stopping, 22, 26, 27
swing, 29
tails, 17
tractor, 24, 25
water, 9, 14, 16, 17, 28, 30
water slide, 28
waterwheel, 14, 15
wheel, 23, 27, 31
wind, 6
wings, 18, 19, 20